YOUR EMOTIONAL ARMOUR

HOW TO DROP IT TO HAVE A HEALTHY RELATIONSHIP

Dr Elena Sherwood

Moody Lane Books,

Greely, Ontario

Canada K4P 1G1

ISBN 978-1-7382702-0-0

www.dr-elena.com

Cover and graphics created in Canva Design Studio, Back Cover photograph by Angela Holmyard

For Reagh.

Contents

Introduction

"Are you sure?" It was 1992, and these were my father's words. "Life is hard enough without you marrying a White, military, protestant man."

Nothing will break us, I thought, *and we aren't weak assholes*!

My red hatchback was loaded with everything I owned, including a bargain wedding dress for whenever and wherever this wedding would be, an Ikea table set, and a plant. I was off to drive 3,500 km to move in with my fiancé in some remote Air Force base. Penniless. Jobless. What I did have was a crisp social work degree, a car that would be mine after 48 more payments, and, of course, the man I love waiting for me.

That was over 30 years ago. We didn't break, but we could have very easily. We've had arguments and harshness all served up without counting the good times in case they didn't balance out. What was the point? No one was leaving. I did ask myself, though: How could we both know in our hearts this marriage is right, but some days everything feels wrong?

In the early 2000s, a few things started to make sense. By then, I was a therapist with a master's degree in couples therapy and a steady stream of distressed relationships coming through my office. I had hunches, but it wasn't until I threw all of myself into my PhD that the biggest exhale of my career and my marriage unfolded.

I was studying healthy marriages and cried the first time I saw us— the kind of relationship we had— described right there on paper and then repeatedly in the studies I read. I had tears of joy, relief, overwhelming pride in what we had unknowingly built, and sorrow for the lost years we would never get back.

It turns out that despite its blemishes, creviced pockmarks, and unsightly red patches, our marriage was, in fact, a very good and healthy one.

My father was wrong. It wasn't skin colour, career, or religion that got in our way. It was how we handled our *emotional armours*; these are walls of sorts that we all craft over time. We put them on as a protective coating. This is where all the troubled relationships I've met stumbled: the marriages in our clinic, the ones in my personal circle, and certainly the one that sleeps in my bed.

You see, at the end of the day, the only things you'll genuinely care about are the things you did or didn't do, the chances you took, and the ones you walked away from. I now know that relationships are riddled with ways to inadvertently damage them, yet bursting with enrichment opportunities that are, unfortunately, rarely seized.

This book is for anyone who's in a romantic relationship, was in one, or plans to be in one. It's a meaningful, practical, and self-reflective read. By the end of this, you'll have some answers to the following questions:

1. Is my relationship healthy?
2. What can I do to have a great relationship?
3. Why do I feel like we're living separate lives?
4. Why is trust so hard?
5. Why can't I get through to him?
6. Why do I feel invisible around her?
7. Why can't we connect?
8. Are relationships supposed to feel this bad?
9. Why do we get so angry at each other sometimes?
10. What can we do to fix us?

11. Is it all my fault we have relationship problems?
12. How do I make him talk?
13. How can I feel freer with my partner?
14. Why am I scared in my relationship?
15. What the hell is even wrong with us?
16. Is my relationship stress "normal"?
17. How can we be better together?
18. Which one of us must change?
19. How do we stop blaming?
20. Why does she do stupid things that hurt me?

The aim of this book is to show you how you put on your emotional armour, why you do it albeit subconsciously, and how to drop it when you must, to let your *the one* in. This powerfully intimate connection is why we bother to have relationships. I assure you that pesky barrier is the last thing you need in what could be a beautiful thing you and your partner have built.

Relationships are supposed to be comforting, grounding, and nurturing, and shouldn't be the major cause of self-doubt, anger, and worry. I want to give you what many of us really wished we'd had. Perhaps what makes this book most unique is the bulk of what you have before you was gathered at the time I was fighting very hard to save my own marriage and didn't even know it.

Chapter One

The ways you protect yourself work against you.

How We Run. When it comes to relationships, the idea of running is evident when you're dating: you pick the unavailable; you don't close off other potential partners while you're with someone; or maybe you find endless reasons, which are really excuses not to go further.

That said, can you run when you're already in a committed and long-term relationship? Married? Oh goodness, yes, that's why we're here.

Let me explain. I'm sure you've met difficult people, the kind who are clueless about how they affect others. They're brick walls you can't get through to, or they're so reactive you upset them, hard as you try not to. Well, here's the mind-bender: mature, calm, and well-adjusted adults can behave like these tiresome folks when it comes to their partners. They, *we*, can find ourselves being unreasonable, defensive, or volatile when it comes to our relationships.

Here are some examples:

1. The high-powered executive who loses her mind when her husband's clothes are on the floor.
2. The successful lawyer who jumps to conclusions when his wife's male colleague sends her a text.

3. The boss who stays at work much later than necessary when his wife is particularly moody.
4. The stockbroker who calls his girlfriend controlling when she tells him his behaviour affects her.
5. The CEO who ignores his wife, sitting right next to him, every evening.
6. The high-profile couple who are the epitome of human physique but are emotionally disconnected from each other.
7. The husband-and-wife sales team who only communicates via heated arguments.
8. The working mom who tells her co-worker about her marital issues but won't talk to her husband about them.
9. The personal trainer who pushes his partner way too hard to get in shape.
10. The woman who goes to bed later to avoid her partner's sexual advances.

We run.

We're masters at justifying why we dodge critical aspects of our relationship, if not the entire thing. Often, we fail to recognize that our actions may not be about moving toward a goal but rather about escaping what awaits us at home. Just to complicate matters, we're often celebrated for how well we do it:

- "Congratulations on your promotion; all that hard work (extra hours) paid off!"

- "Damn, are those washboard abs?"

- "I don't know how they do it, doing it all, having it all! I wish I knew their secret."

Sometimes, the running is guided by ideas we've been taught or picked up along the way which we rigidly hang onto:

- "Men are all the same."
- "Women are just so emotional."
- "I suck at relationships."
- "Of course he messed up, typical."
- "Marriages don't last."
- "I'm not the problem; my partner is."
- "He's just clueless and incapable!"
- "I knew she was going to let me down. That's what women do."
- "It's all my fault, I'm damaged."
- "Bad relationships run in my family."

Let's face it, most relationships can have fantastic beginning phases where we temporarily lower our guards, just enough for our partner to see hints of our real selves. That's what we all crave on a primal level: genuine, unobstructed, and unadulterated connection. Unfortunately, somewhere in the whirlwind of expectations and demands, couples go wayward, never quite getting to, or staying in, that coveted sacred zone of what relationships are *really* about. It's heartbreaking to watch couples take each other for granted, assuming that finding the one is the only goal. It is not.

Let me be *very* clear. The ultimate goal of every relationship is to get close; you are to lay down your swords, drop your protective shields, and let each other in. Then, you are to push to get closer yet. You don't do that by "keeping the peace", but by understanding each other even better over time; through constant and continued sorting, even re-sorting of *all* that arises.

What exactly do I mean by close? I mean *vulnerable* close; I mean *if I lost you, my heart would shatter into a million pieces* close, and *I will build my entire life around what we have because, together, we ARE a home, and it's so safe and so powerful it's beyond comprehension* close. There, you'll also find unlimited motivation to *fight* for it; it becomes indestructible because you decide to make it so. As you may know or have guessed, the journey there is unnerving, the risks are enormous, and the stakes sky high.

What's the difference between this level of closeness and co-dependency? Being co-dependent is about relying too much on your partner to make you *feel* okay, *be* okay, or vice versa. The lines there are blurred. Healthy intimate closeness isn't about becoming enmeshed or overtaxed, because here, no one carries anyone, nor is that desired. This means walking side-by-side with someone who truly cares about your well-being, each strengthening who you are individually, and creating an enriched and solid bond without ever losing yourself.

Is the arduous path to this kind of intimacy worth it? The research is indisputable. Healthy relationships have been known to help people live longer, heal faster, have greater overall life satisfaction, and have the guidance of a well-defined purpose (Waldinger and Schulz, 2010). Research shows that healthy marriages benefit those involved (Don et al., 2023; Waite and Gallagher, 2001).

If you're wondering if such things exist in real life outside of these studies, I assure you they are everywhere! It's your neighbour's relationship, your accountant's, the store manager's where you buy groceries, or that of the couple sitting at the back in your favorite coffee shop, speaking to each other with indescribable familiarity in their eyes. If you ask them what their secrets are, they'll gladly tell you because they want you to have what they enjoy every day.

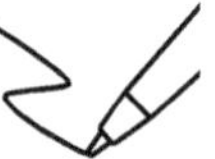

Journal Prompt:

Did I run from others in the past? If so, how?

Chapter Two

The truths that matter most are the ones you tell yourself.

Why You Run. So far, I've told you about how partners run from each other. Now, let's talk about why. All these pieces are connected so bear with me.

If you want to clearly understand your relationship, you must see that it's the sum of its parts: there are only two. Together, you've created something. You each brought whatever you have, all that you know, to create your *us*, all of which was influenced and shaped by your personal stories.

This is where we zoom in on you, just you for now, to get a closer look. You and the way you see the world are also the sum of your parts, which are your insights based on the life you've led thus far. You draw upon these all the live-long day and even at night as you sleep. You do this automatically in the undercurrent of your awareness, and it's as natural as breathing. So, to understand why you do what you do in your relationship, you begin by understanding how *you* see the world. To do that, we'll need your story.

When I tell someone it's time to look at their past, I'm often met with resistance. Sometimes, they outright argue with me, and here are the usual protests:

1. "I've had an easy life; I wasn't abused or anything, so there's no need to look back." Everyone has a complex and multi-layered story, regardless of how simple it may appear.

2. "What's in the past should stay there." Your mind and body lived through it and still carry its effects.

3. "My parents did their best, so I'm not interested in blaming them." We aren't looking to blame but merely to understand; your parents had their own stories that came into play one way or another while they were raising *you*.

4. "I've done a lot of inner work; I've rewritten my own story, so this doesn't apply to me." Having a healed view of your past doesn't erase the way it unfolded, and having a healthier mental condition today doesn't mean you can *un-know*.

5. "I'm not here for individual work; I want to fix my marriage." What you say and do in your marriage depends a lot on your beliefs, as well as how those have come to be.

The following diagram is a snapshot of what I want you to see about yourself right now. The small circles are groupings of experiences that affect how your sense of self was loosely formed.

You are far more sophisticated than this, but this gives you a place to start looking at some of the most meaningful parts of you that you may not think about too often.

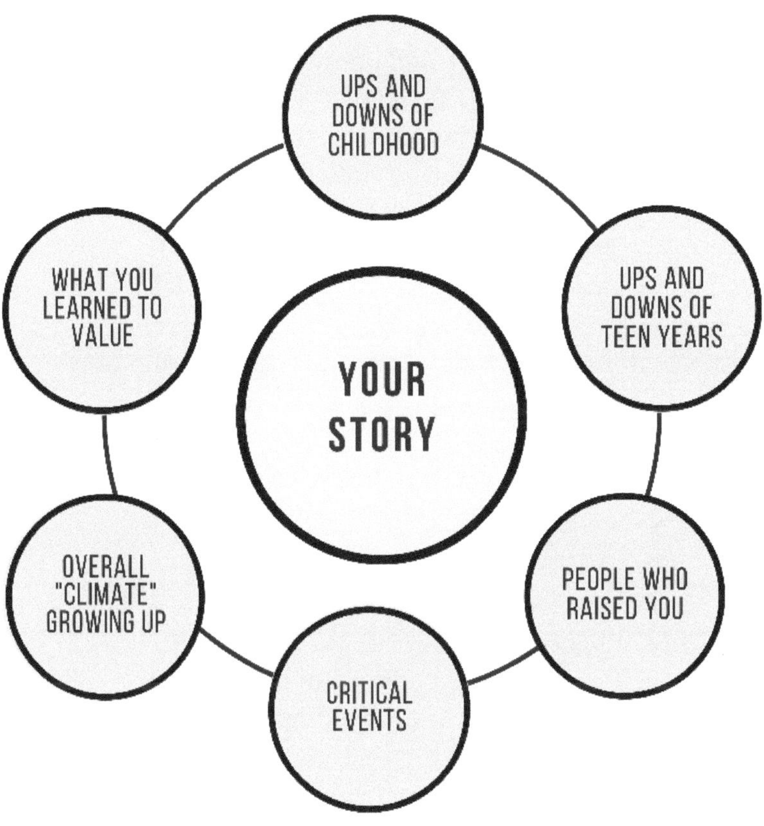

FIGURE 1 – YOU

We're focusing on all these parts of you for three very important reasons:

1. To remind you that a lot happened in your life well before your current relationship began.

2. It's near impossible to recall every occurrence that is relevant to your life-view formation, even the good ones, on your own.

3. These life-changing moments and their effects are directing what you do in your relationship today; it's best you know what's driving *you*.

In the following pages, you'll find questions that let you peek behind your own curtain, where you've learned to make sense of, deal with, and protect yourself as your life happened. If you want to get the most out of reading this short book, I urge you to answer every single one of them. Do take your time; you weren't built overnight, and neither was everything you've come to believe.

Grab a pen and notebook so you can really immerse yourself; type them out if you must, but handwriting does a better job of connecting you more with this kind of deeply personal content.

Section 1: Ups and Downs of Childhood

1. What's your earliest memory?

2. What feelings did you experience?

3. What's it like for you now, thinking of this memory today?

4. Who was there?

5. Where were you living?

Section 2: Those Who Raised You

1. What were the people who raised you like?

2. Did they have strong or unremarkable personality traits?

3. Were they solid and grounded, or do you think they had unmet needs back then?

4. Would you say they were physically present enough?

5. What about their emotional presence? Was that enough?

6. How did they treat you?

7. How is your relationship with them now?

8. How did they affect your self-image?
   a) They helped me feel good about myself.
   b) They damaged my self-image.
   c) I still don't know.
   d) Other:

Section 3: What You Learned to Value

1. What did those who raised you want you to value (for example, religion, money, education, appearance, or others)?

2. Did you agree with their beliefs then?

3. What do you think of those beliefs now?

4. Did their beliefs come with expectations of you?

5. Did you feel invisible and insignificant, or treasured and loved?

6. Would you/do you raise your children differently?

7. Other important details?

Section 4: Overall Climate

1. If you were to use the word "climate" to describe how your home environment felt growing up, which description fits best?
   a) Warm, cozy, and comfortable
   b) Tepid, lukewarm at best

> c) Lonely, cool, or cold
> d) Other:

2. Did this change at all over time for you? If so, what changed it, and how?

Section 5: Ups and Downs of Teen Years

1. Adolescence can be exciting, disorienting, and/or confusing. Did you have the guidance you needed to navigate the physical changes?

2. What about the emotional/psychological changes?

3. What were your relationships with your parents/caregiver like then (choose one)?
   a) It was healthy; I felt their support.
   b) It was strained.
   c) I raised myself.

4. Did you have close friends during your teens?

5. Did you want to belong?

6. Did you rebel?

7. Did you hide, or did you shine?

8. Other?

9. How did you feel in your teen years overall?
   a) Truly confident
   b) Scattered
   c) Lonely
   d) Numb

Section 6: Critical Events

1. What events significantly impacted you? These are things like moves, losses, death, separation, change in family make up, illness, injuries, traumas, natural disasters, among others.

2. How did your parent(s)/caregiver cope?

3. How did you cope?

4. Think about how you felt overall growing up, choose one from each of the following:
   a) Powerless or Empowered
   b) Unsafe or Safe
   c) Anxious or Calm
   d) Forgotten or Valued
   e) Insecure or Competent

If you've done a cursory scan of the questions, I'm glad you're planting the seed of their relevance in the back of your mind; please make sure to come back to them.

If you're resisting or simply unwilling to go there right now, take a break and revisit these later.

If you feel ready to throw away or delete this book, may I suggest you take the time to reflect on why that is? It may help to see a mental health professional.

If you're passionately committed to making changes and have answered every question, well done!

I must draw your attention to an eye-opening pattern that emerged in my decades of work: *when it comes to your relationship, the important parts aren't what you think.* You will have noticed I didn't ask if your parents divorced, or if you grew up homeless. Like my father, we are quick to assume or blame certain demographics.

It's critical you know that when it comes to your relationship, you and your partner stand as equals, regardless of what either of you believe are disadvantages based on your personal histories. *As you will learn throughout this book, the defining factor lies in what you do with your emotional armour.*

The questions here served as a reminder that somewhere on your way to your partner, you lived a very full life. Despite the good, there were moments where you felt *abandoned*, *rejected*, and/or *dismissed*. Life does that to us. These particular three are the bane of everyone's existence when it comes to relationships even when we don't realize it.

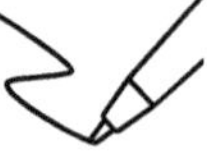

Journal Prompt:

Do I like visiting my past?

What was this chapter like for me?

Chapter Three

The fear of pain is one unwieldy beast.

Emotional Armour. In the first two chapters, I've shown you how you run and why. Here is where emotional armour comes in: we are shaped by characters, events, and experiences, and our personal stories stay with us as we enter our current relationship. We bring in all we've been carrying, the whole stylish matching luggage set, along with everything tucked away in its hidden compartments. Blissful as love can be, the deep cuts, however healed they are, have left their mark and they are right where we left them. We keep a mental tally of the awful things we've survived, whether we realize it or not. Here's the real kicker: pain, especially the kind that hasn't really been dealt with or processed into manageable sizes, has a way of dirtying clean things.

Let's have a good look at what healthy relationships are. They're the kind where two people choose each other repeatedly, always until death, or unless one does exceptionally dumb things. Even then, some find their way back to each other. These relationships are the furthest things from perfect, yet they work. They enhance the lives of those in them and around them. They're understated, subdued, and draw little attention to themselves because such a union knows what it needs, and it doesn't come from anything outside of itself.

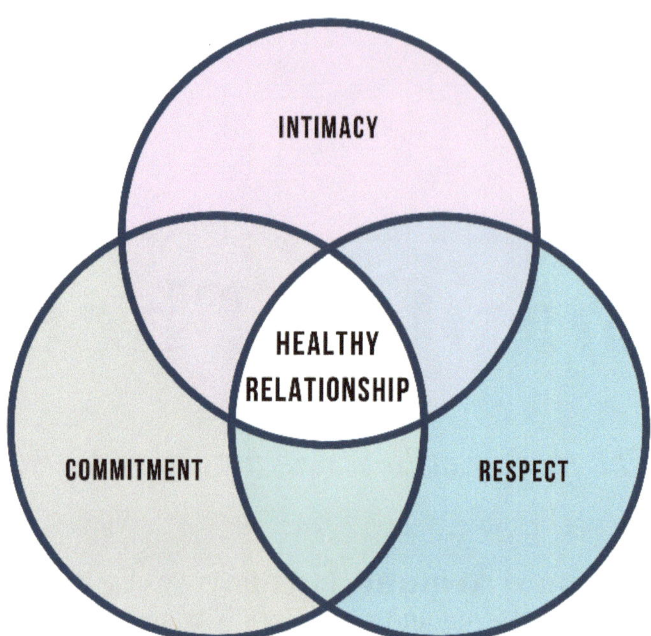

FIGURE 2 - HEALTHY RELATIONSHIPS

Healthy relationships are built on three solid foundations: they have intimacy, as in there's a deep want and desire for two people to be with each other in a dedicated and exclusive way; they have commitment, where they don't quit on each other or the relationship just because it gets tough; and they have respect, wherein they value all that is their partner, including the parts they don't like. Simple as these components may seem, they really are not.

In the previous chapter, I reminded you that somewhere in all of us, we know the stings of rejection, abandonment, and dismissal. Here, I just talked about intimacy, commitment, and respect. These groupings of three are opposites! To love someone deeply means you risk being pushed away (intimacy vs. rejection); when you're all-in, you know your partner could leave (committed vs. abandoned); and instead of being valued, there's a chance your partner will make you feel small or insignificant (respect vs. dismissal).

Here is a very personal example of what I mean, and to be honest, it's still not easy to relive this moment three decades later. This was our first fall together in our stuffy, low-budget, two-bedroom apartment in the isolated north.

"I need more clean socks," my then fiancé mumbled in frustration, rummaging through drawers in the dark as he got ready to go to work. We'd been living together for two months; I was still jobless; my last paycheck and relevant paperwork were lost in the mail, so I couldn't file for unemployment benefits, or as my mom called it, "welfare."

We were watching every cent and had no idea how we'd be paying for our spring wedding. His words hit me in mid-thought: somewhere between, *is it too soon to call my best friend back home again, I don't want to depress her with my pity parties* and, *I hate that I cried on our last call, no...no, I will not cry right now. Nope. Not today.*

Wrapped tightly under the polyblend covers that were failing me, I froze at his words. I stared at the frost on the window and the dark, bleakness beyond. "What the...I'm not your maid. I wasn't put on this planet to serve you. WASH YOUR OWN SHIT!" I snapped.

Taken aback, he replied, "I didn't mean...I...you know what, I'll do it when I get home. It's no big deal, really."

"Yeah, coz THAT makes a lot of sense," I said bitingly. "By the time you get home, I will have WASHED your clothes, CLEANED this place, and COOKED your supper. HAPPY NOW?"

He sat still on his side of the bed. Military members can't be late, so there was no time to deal with my sarcasm or whatever was beneath it; I heard a suppressed sigh as he finished getting ready and left for work.

How is this my life? I thought. *How did I go from having a chic apartment on Yonge Street in a trendy part of Toronto with my own*

*income and a membership to the snazzy gym overlooking brilliant city
lights, surrounded by friends and family, to this?*

I was exhausted; I'd been trying to make friends, even cold-called a
woman I casually met, but she didn't want me; no one did. I'd been
plastering a bright, cheery smile on my face as I dropped off resumes
where the recipients barely looked up. Then another thought hit me,
*the brutal cold winter is just around the corner, and I have tropical
fucking blood.*

I burrowed further under the covers, squeezing my eyes shut. Then, I
failed at my one goal for the day because the silent tears came.

Just like that, we humans go from 0 to 900 degrees in nanoseconds,
and we don't even know we've done it. At the moment, I was hurting,
and I didn't care that now he was hurting too, and it started with me.
Perhaps I was clinically depressed, which could've made it
understandable but not excusable. Nope. Even in that state, I was
responsible for my actions. We all are. We always are.

For me, I was set off by a man telling me to do his laundry, even if I
knew he was the kindest and most respectful person I'd ever met and
still is. This was one of the many reasons I chose to marry him, his
uncanny way of making me feel seen and heard.

Maybe for you, it will be dirty dishes, a tasteless joke, or a careless
gesture that will make you snap. Perhaps instead of yelling, you'll pull
away, swallow your pain, store your anger, or spin yourself into a
perfect storm. We can and do assume the worst when we're
emotionally triggered. We jump to conclusions. We fill in the blanks
with whatever we're compelled to. Then suddenly, we're armoured
up, withdrawing, or attacking with defenses that are fully engaged.
That's the crap we all pull in relationships. We don't do it to be our
partner's royal pain in the butt; we do it because we're *human.*

Did you know that your partner, your *the one,* might very well be the
person you protect yourself from the most? When you really think

about it, we don't usually behave irrationally with acquaintances, colleagues, or even our good friends. All these other people are in our orbits, after all, so why wouldn't we unleash upon them or freeze them out the way we more readily do towards our partners?

Here's the thing: somewhere along the way, your significant other got through your Fort Knox security system. You allowed them in. You've said, "I love you," you've shared a bed, you are sharing a life and you've visualized a future. You've accepted *emotional proximity,* which is the specific kind of closeness that happens when two people basically hand each other their hearts, albeit shakily. You've entrusted your partner with the power and breadth to cherish it with reverence, or to kick it to the curb with steel-toed boots.

Remember, your partner is also the sum of their parts, so whatever inner chaos you experience in this nearness, they have their own version of this, swirling inside of them too.

What did decades in this field teach me about the leading causes of breakups, separation, and divorce? It's *loneliness* in the relationship. It doesn't take much to widen the gap between the two of you. There are many roads to loneliness, and some are more subtle. It could be in the way we expect our partners to shape themselves, maybe just a little or a whole lot, yet we ignore their pleas for us to do the same.

Other roads to loneliness are in things like:

- a holier-than-thou tone
- when words are poorly delivered and never corrected
- how what's said was grossly misunderstood and yet no clarifying questions were asked
- the apologies that weren't made, the angered and explosive conversation that led to silence, the silence that built walls, and the walls that turn into fortresses.

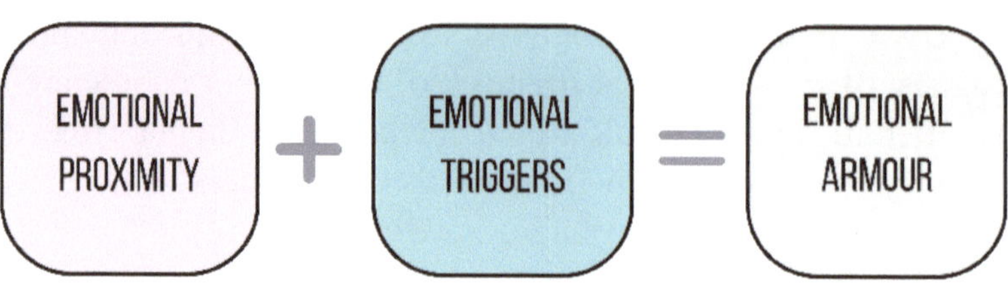

FIGURE 3 - THE THREE ES

Here is an equation that explains the process. I've talked about these three Es for very good reasons: the mere fact that you have someone very close to you (emotional proximity) is emotionally triggering. By this I mean at times, it will feel a little *too close,* or perhaps it will look like your partner is pulling away from you, so you armour up in case they decide to leave. You'll convince yourself you need to protect yourself, even when you really don't. This isn't a cautionary act like grabbing an umbrella because the clouds are heavy; it's more like putting on full rain gear, from double-sided bucket hat down to galoshes, on a clear sunny day.

If you take hold of how these concepts are interacting with each other, OWN them, and grasp how they apply to YOU, how your relationship *feels* and *functions* will shift. Exponentially. Dramatically. Exaltingly. How you receive, perceive, and approach your partner will set you on the path to the level of closeness I discussed earlier, towards true relationship success.

I've laid all this out before you to remind you that despite your whys and hows, you are not a hapless being to be pulled willy-nilly in all directions, nor are you at the mercy of your next painful, triggered exchange. You have choices. You have the means and wherewithal to do things differently. If others can, and they have, so can you.

Here's another personal example. This one shows you how seemingly subtle, yet unmistakable emotional armouring can be. At this point, we'd been married for three years and living in our cozy first home:

"Wanna hear this?" I asked my husband. "I think I finally nailed the chords." He was walking past our bedroom, so he came to join me on the bed, where I sat with old songbooks and an even older guitar. I'd been wrestling with the sappy ballad called "Love is All Around You." I'd never sung to him, to anyone, so I did my best.

I pushed myself all the way through to the last line about pleading for love to be shown, then gently trailing off. I let out a cleansing breath. The vulnerability of the whole experience had me a little choked up in parts, so I blinked away the moisture in my eyes.

I looked at him, only to watch him do the last thing I'd ever expected. Without glancing my way, he stood up, faced the door, and walked out silently.

What the hell was that? Did he seriously just…leave? I thought.

I sat still for several moments. Confused and out of sorts, I followed him; I found him in the living room, leafing through a book but clearly not reading it.

"Um, what did you think of it? Why'd you just...go?" I asked.

With a pained look in his eyes, he replied, "It…was good."

"Stung a bit that you just left," I responded.

"I didn't do that to hurt you. I don't know why I did it. I still don't," he said softly, returning to his non-reading.

Similar things happened a few more times, and then one day, he managed to put his thoughts and feelings into words: "When you give me really big gifts, I worry that I'll never give you as much back. What if I can't? What if I'm not enough for you? That terrifies me."

Again, just like that. There was a night and day shift for both of us when he connected his reaction to a hidden fear. Without it I would've continued believing he rejects and dismisses me when I really open up to him, which was inaccurate. His response to the song was proof that he does let me in, to the point that he didn't know what to do with the mixed feelings. From then on, I knew what to expect in future intimate moments, and that has helped us both.

Emotional proximity, which is really *intimacy,* will trigger you. It won't make sense, yet you'll pull away with a knee-jerk reaction. This is why it can be hard to be the first to say I love you, or why you fret when it isn't said right back. Even if they say it right back you may wonder if they did so out of obligation. This may be why you hesitate to give a genuine compliment, or why you downplay one with *that's what you're supposed to say.* This is why we want to hide our flaws and insecurities, because what if we scare them away?

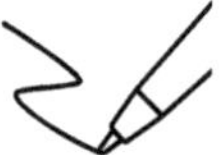

Journal Prompt:

Does my partner believe I open up easily (ask them)?

Is opening up hard for me, if so, why?

Chapter Four

Deal with the shadows by befriending what makes them.

Moving forward. How on earth can all this help you and your relationship? To break out of this destructive relationship push and pull, I'll let you in on the overarching game plan I formed through the years. It's in three concrete and well-worth-it steps, which is the most direct path I can find to get you shifting. I know they aren't easy, but they are doable. Here's how:

1. You learn how to tell you're emotionally triggered the moment it happens.

2. You narrow down your kryptonite areas, so to speak, by identifying what *specific* things make you upset.

3. You get to know what your go-to *protection tactics* are, which are your weapons of choice when you feel threatened in your relationship.

Over time and with practice, these three steps get easier and easier to do. So, grab that notebook again and write down everything that you sense applies to you with regards to all you're about to read.

Understanding You, Triggered.

When you're amid a reaction, your words could be tangled and elusive. However, your body never lies, so here are some of the physical signs you will experience:

- Your heartbeat is racing.
- You sense a sudden drop in mood.
- You feel generally unsafe.
- You are clenching fists, teeth, or jaw.
- Your head feels hot.
- Details around you fade a little, or they become more pronounced than normal.
- Your gut is knotted or churning.
- There's a lump in your throat.
- You are the only one in the room reacting.
- You might find it difficult to breathe.

These are in the same ballpark as generalized anxiety symptoms. In fact, they've led to full-blown panic attacks for some, but for most of us, it ranges anywhere from being uncomfortable to feeling openly tortured.

A triggered moment is instantaneous and all-consuming; we don't usually have all the time in the world nor the expansive mental awareness to know what we are experiencing. If we were able to though, here are some of the words we'd use to name what we're going through at the time:

Abandoned * Afraid * Angry * Attacked * Belittled * Betrayed Brutalized * Cast Aside * Confused * Dehumanized * Demoralized Defensive * Dejected * Demeaned * Devalued * Discarded

Disempowered * Dismissed * Disoriented * Disregarded Disrespected * Enraged * Forgotten * Frustrated * Furious * Guarded Harmed * Helpless * Hopeless * Humiliated * Hurt * Ignored Incensed * Insignificant * Insulted * Invisible * Left Behind * Less Than * Livid * Lonely * Lost * Minimized * Mortified * Petrified Powerless * Rageful * Rejected * Repulsed * Saddened * Shamed Terrified * Terrorized * Threatened * Trapped * Violated * Undone Unloved * Undervalued * Unworthy * Used * Weak * Weakened Worthless

These are just some of what I've seen, but of course, there are hundreds of others. The important thing is that *you* find words that best resonate with what you're feeling.

Understanding Your Kryptonite.

If you haven't noticed yet, this book is very much centred on sharpening your innate ability to be self-aware. Healthy relationships are only possible when we cease looking at what our partner's issues are, and deliberately examine our own (if you're with a diagnosable narcissist or a mentally cruel partner I encourage you to look for local supports right away.)

Everyone has buttons that will get pressed, meaning, when you look hard enough, you'll see there are certain kinds of things that put you on high alert. If you go back to Chapter Two, where I nudged you toward your story, you will have found some of those sensitive spots. Please revisit those answers now.

1. Which areas of questioning were toughest for you?

2. Which ones did you ignore or want to ignore?

3. Which ones made you angry or sad?

If you recall, I ended that chapter with the trio of abandonment, rejection, and dismissal because we are most raw when it comes to one, or unfortunately, all three of these. I'll be upfront and tell you they are all my archenemies. Anything that can be twisted to look like those set off my mental alarm, so much so that I wrote about them. My first book was about my sordid immigration story, and this is the foreword written by an esteemed colleague: "…the parent-child relationship, the ways children protect themselves, and the flawed adult these experiences form…" (Sherwood & Dean, 2021, p 2.)

Flawed, I am, as we all are. I wasn't abused. My parents didn't drink, and they were married for 47 years upon my mother's death. They were of sound mind, rational, and conscientious, yet I have scars just like yours, as did they.

None of us go unscathed. We make assumptions about why people become guarded; the truth is, one way or another, we all end up here: overly careful when it comes to our hearts. Everyone does.

The sooner we wrap our brains around *how* we harm our relationships and, ultimately, our partners in our pursuit of this mythical ever-so-safe bubble, the better life gets for everyone involved.

Understanding Your Tactics.

I invite you to consider how you deal with your partner when you're triggered. If you're unsure, then show your partner this list because when it comes to armouring up, here are the usual ways people "cope." Note which one of these you do, and see if your partner agrees:

The Silent Treatment.

This could be simply refusing to speak, ignoring texts/calls, or responding with one-word answers. I've seen it used for three reasons:

To Manage Feelings. Sometimes when there's too much going on one partner can get emotionally overwhelmed, leading to a strong desire to shut all conversations down. If you fall into this category, make sure to tell your partner that you need a mental pause. It may help to play or listen to music that rhymes with what's happening inside you. Spend time journaling, have a look at the earlier list in Chapter Two and name your feelings. Ask yourself the following:

"What am I feeling that confirms I'm triggered?"
"Why am I triggered?"
"What am I most afraid of right now when it comes to my partner?"
"Could this be about my past and not my present?"

Be meaningful about regaining balance with several deep breaths. Make sure to have another conversation with your partner no more than a day later, even if it's only to *agree to disagree* for now. Reconvening within 24 hours is critical, because it will prevent the situation from getting out of hand. The point, after all, is to work *through* the issues.

When Feeling Unheard. When you're with someone who is unable or unwilling to listen, going silent seems like the easiest solution; it may seem like the only one. There is often a *why bother, what's the point of speaking when it falls on deaf ears* way of thinking here, and understandably so. If this is you, consider saying the following: "For some reason we aren't getting through to each other right now. Can we slow this conversation down a little? Tell me what you need me to hear, and I'll tell you what I need you to hear, can we try that?" Be kind to yourselves on this front because effective communication takes time and practice; most of us aren't naturally born good listeners with the ability to absorb everything being given to us. It's essential you both *try* to transmit your message and try to *receive each other's accurately*. Your partner doesn't know what you misunderstood, so you must tell them (there will be more additional tools later).

To Assert Power/Control. If using *the silent treatment* is your way of punishing or teaching your partner a lesson, I must tell you this: you are actively destroying your relationship. Creating some sort of power imbalance leaves your partner feeling small or less than, and those who feel that way in the relationship tend to fall into depression or suffer from anxiety. It's likely they are questioning whether they should stay, and if this happens too often, they will leave when they figure out how. It will be helpful for you to remember that your partner is your equal. We cannot and must not expect our equals to bend to our will and spend their living days doing and saying what we want. If you can't stop yourself from using silence to "deal" with your partner, it may be time to seek professional help.

Avoiding Conflict

Maybe you learned to avoid conflict at all costs, to the point that you hold in your real thoughts, feelings, or opinions; avoidance is different from the *silent treatment* because you do talk, but you make yourself agreeable, often concede, or are selective about what you say to avoid minefields. This is harmful to you because you aren't being authentic, and you are suppressing the very parts of you that make you unique. This is also exhausting. When I worked at a mental health clinic, we often received referrals from exasperated physicians who've run out of ways to help their depressed or anxious patients. Inauthenticity leads to physical illness. If this is you, it would be helpful for you to dig deep into what conflict means to you and write out what you think the worst-case scenarios are. What are your greatest fears when it comes to conflict in your relationship? Do those fears make sense? Are they reasonable?

Being Passive-Aggressive

This entails saying one thing but doing another; for example, you may carry on as if everything's fine, but you do things like talk about your partner behind their back, you may underhandedly "forget" to do something that matters to them, or you may keep secrets as a way of getting back at them as subconscious or conscious act of defiance. If this is you, I encourage you to explore *why* you don't use your voice. Think about the following questions: Is this about being afraid of conflict? Is this related to you feeling unheard when you do speak? Might you be feeling like your opinion isn't as valuable or important as your partner's?

If your partner has toxic traits like constantly belittling you, making everything your fault, dismisses you outwardly and has no desire to change their behaviour, then here are urgent questions to ask yourself: "Is this what I deserve?" "Is this really the life I want for myself?" "Is this the life I'd want for my children, or for someone I care about?"

Rationalizing or Excusing

This one is centered around a person who is unwilling to hold themself accountable or won't accept responsibility for their words or actions. There will always be endless "reasons" one can draw on to make excuses for their behaviour. You were tired, that's why you snapped at your partner. Your friends pressure you into drinking too much. Your mother needs you, so you must leave at the *exact* moment your partner wants to talk. That project is so important that it demands *all* your time, energy, and focus. Your boss is demanding, so you don't have the bandwidth for relationship issues.

This is your reminder that important as you are, you are 50 percent of the relationship, so you must carry your weight in the problem-solving domain. Not only are you putting additional stress on your partner by making them chase you, but you're also expecting them to handle two-person tasks on their own. The fix here is to admit, first to yourself and then to your partner, that rationalizing and excusing are things you sometimes do. Make concerted efforts to catch the moments you are ready to defend, then pause. Another option is to give your partner full permission to call you out on this unhealthy tactic and make a pact to accept this from them even when you'd rather not (unfortunately with this you run the risk of yet again, relying on someone else to fix things, so use this with caution).

Accusing, Blaming, Attacking, Threatening

Too much of this is damaging in the long run because you can get stuck in launch mode, rendering you unable to hear your partner's perspective. This pushes your partner away, making your relationship a breeding ground for mistrust and miscommunication. Unresolved issues compound over time. To curtail this, make it a point to remember that your partner is your *partner*, not your enemy, and that you're in this relationship by choice. It's useful to zoom out of your emotional head by pausing to reflect on the words you just said, and the way you just said them. Ask yourself this: Do I listen, really listen, as much as I talk, do I treat my partner the way I want to be treated?

Leaving

Taking a bit of a break is understandable, and sometimes it's exactly what a couple needs to figure out what's happening, how they're reacting, and what they're reacting to. This one must come with a giant USE WITH CAUTION warning for two critical reasons: leaving sets a person up to fall into doing this habitually, which may start with small exits but over time turn into one's default way of coping. The second caution is it can easily look and feel like abandonment to the person left behind, especially to a partner who's sustained multiple losses or even just one terribly painful one. I suggest that when things are calm, have an adult conversation about the following guidelines to avoid senseless heartache:

1. This is NOT a relationship break where it's now okay to see other people or connect with others in an emotionally cheating manner.
2. Out of respect you'll always let the other one know where you are and be reachable in case of an emergency.
3. You will re-connect, even by text, within 24 hours.

Becoming An Island

This includes withdrawing, believing you don't really need anyone, not even your partner, and you can fix everything yourself. Perhaps you do this to keep a safe distance between you, especially if you're particularly sensitive to abandonment. You do this to ensure that if your partner did leave, it would hurt less, or so you think. Firstly, it won't. In fact, you'll make the situation worse because you'll realize that your wall *was* a big reason the relationship ended. Secondly, regardless of your reasoning, this makes it uncomfortable for your partner to be around you because there's a surface-only feel to your relationship. The way forward here is about accepting that your partner loves you and desires closeness from you, as much as you yourself desire from them whether you admit it or don't. That's why you're together. Yes, it's white-knuckle terrifying, but that's only one part of what you both have together. Your partner is terrified too.

Withholding Affection or Manipulation

This is different from being an island because holding back here is premised on the assertion of power and control. It's like using *the silent treatment*, but this is globally and intentionally withholding what you know your partner needs, craves or desires. If you do this, this is unhealthy because you are only interested in meeting your needs and will do whatever you want for it.

There is no equation in the history of intimate relationships, where withholding love is a good thing. None. If you do this, you likely wouldn't be reading this book, but if you are, please seek professional help. I'm also mentioning this in case you see these damaging and very dangerous characteristics in your relationship. If you do, understand now that this has grave consequences for your whole being; I urge you to seek a qualified therapist and other support. Immediately.

Look for Emotional Armour in:

1. The way you hold a grudge.
2. The impatience in your tone.
3. The volume of your voice.
4. Your disappointed look.
5. How you shut down conversations.
6. The way you turn your back.
7. Your condescending stance.
8. Your refusal to listen.
9. How you have an answer for everything.
10. The way you speak without saying much.

11. How you pull away.
12. The physical distance you keep.
13. Your critical tone.
14. The excuses you make.
15. Your endless blaming.
16. Your death grip on your own opinion.
17. How you avoid apologizing.
18. How you ignore their pleas.
19. Your growing list of everything they've done wrong.
20. The way you withhold affection.

Understanding your triggered self, your kryptonite, and your tactics knock the wind out of relationship drama's sail. Triggers lose their intensity, and armours lower. It helps you step back enough to observe yourself. You gain clarity. It softens you. It helps you tap into the mature adult you are. You'll see conflict lose its fizz, and it can turn into points of connection, deeper knowing, and personal growth.

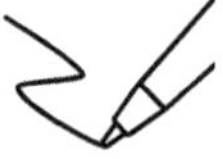

Journal Prompt:

What do I do when my partner upsets me?

What did I learn about myself in this chapter?

Chapter Five

Relationship surety is earned.

Now what? Can you imagine a relationship wherein having a reaction inside of you leads to closeness between the two of you? Where emotional proximity shifts from being threatening to becoming *intimate?*

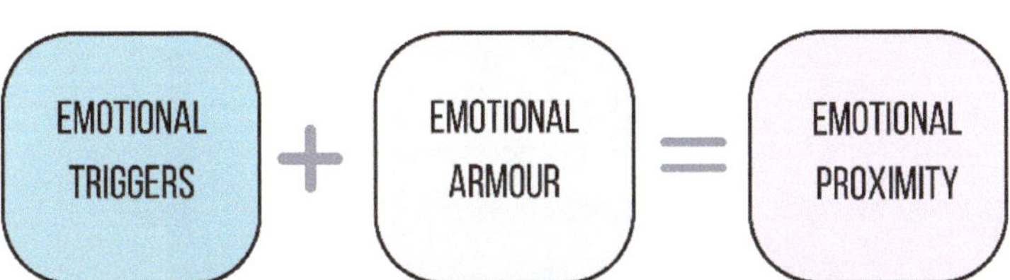

FIGURE 4 - EMOTIONAL PROXIMITY

The three Es are the same here, but the equation has been rearranged from working against you to working *for* you. When you and your partner manage to share what you know about yourselves in the heat of the moment, or just after, this turns down the intensity, thus making room for a healthy and relating conversation.

How To Use:

Let's have a look back at the first personal example I shared, where I lost it over the "I need more socks" statement and apply what we've talked about so far. If I'd known then what I know now about emotional triggers, this is the way things could have gone instead.

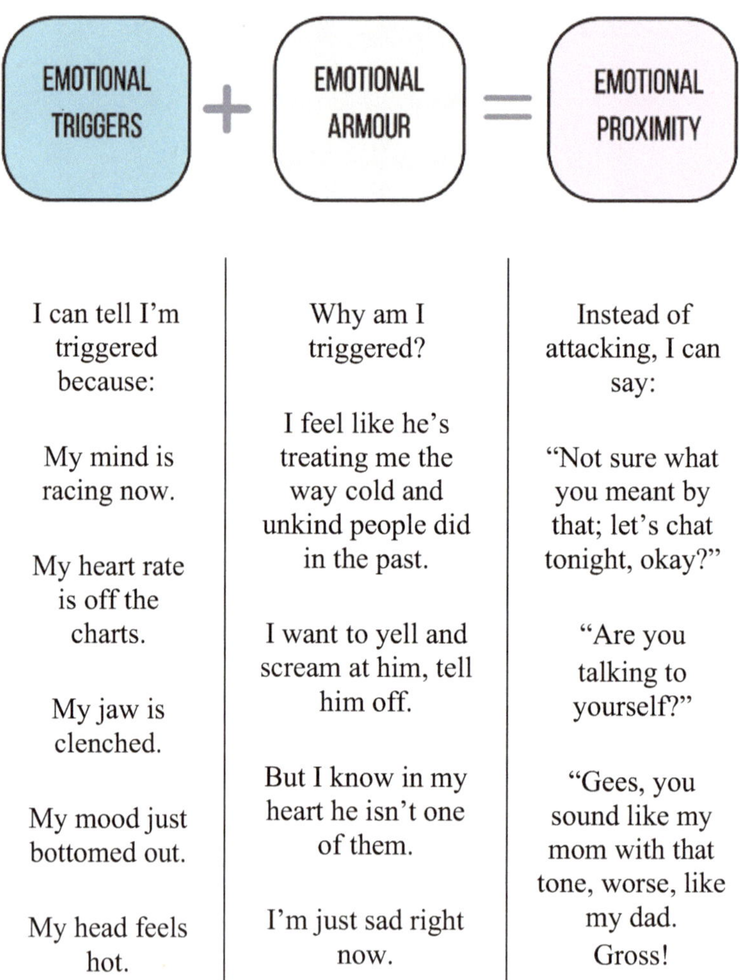

Now its time to tie all this together! So, here is an over-simplified, sped up for your convenience, fictional couple that personifies the thousands of scenarios I have faced in my practice.

Jen and Mark

Jen is a 28-year-old occupational therapist who has been married to Mark, a 29-year-old architect for the last five years. The live in a cozy suburban home.

The biggest issue they presented with was about children. Jen was ready to have them, and has been for the last three years, but Mark wanted to save more money and have a solid footing in his career. They've had several talks about this, the last heated discussion did not go well, such that Jen stormed out and spent the weekend with her best friend a few blocks over. This was two weeks ago; Jen indicated that neither her nor Mark have spoken much since she returned. They proceeded to stay away from anything beyond "pass the salt" to avoid fighting. Jen convinced Mark to come for a few couple therapy sessions before they drift too far apart. Despite hesitation, he agreed.

Using the diagrams and questions throughout this book, the deeper issues related to emotional proximity, emotional triggers and emotional armour were examined, thus revealing what was under the surface.

How they run.

Since their impasse Mark has been spending evenings in the basement working on his hobbies or at the gym. Jen crocheted, read, or watched TV in the living room, avoiding going downstairs.

Mark had been coming to bed only when he was certain Jen was asleep. Jen on the other hand had been getting up early and leaving for work before Mark got to his morning coffee.

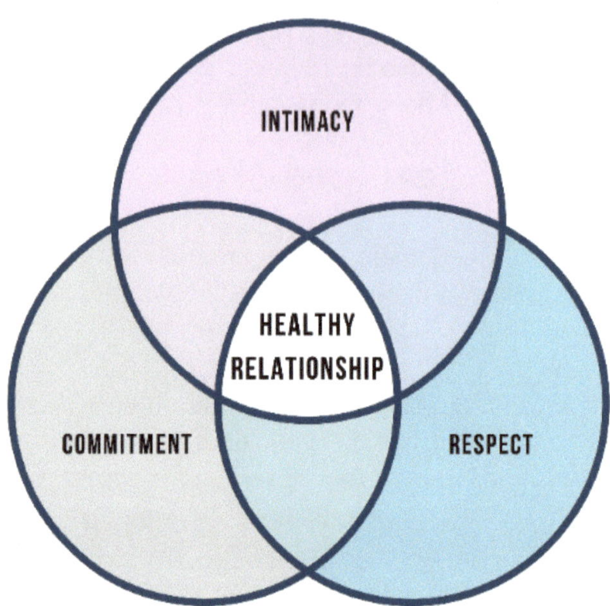

Despite their current issues, it became clear right away that their marriage was strong. Intimacy was clear in their body language; Jen tended to lean towards Mark's chair, which seemed to be out of concern for how he was doing in the session. Mark, as soon as they entered, pulled his chair closer to his wife's, and reached for her hand several times.

They were committed. They declared at the onset that there was no interest in separating or even time apart. Mark thanked Jen for taking the space she needed, because he hadn't realized he too needed the mental pause as well until after she'd left.

While there were some moments of heightened emotion and strong words, there was without a doubt, a distinct element of respect. It was clear that both were experiencing a lot of difficult feelings, but they made the effort to focused on the issues at hand.

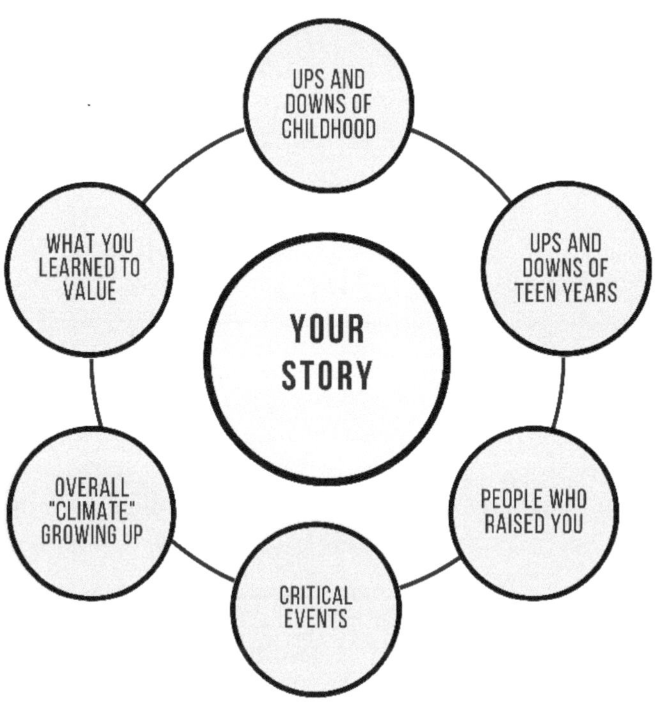

Jen

Section 1: Ups and Downs of Childhood

Jen was the oldest of two girls. Her earliest memory was of being three years old, looking at her newborn sister Sue sleeping in a crib. She remembered feeling strange, maybe it was confusion, but she couldn't recall why. The room was dark, her parents were standing on the other side of the crib shushing her.

Jen remembered her mom gripping a yellow handkerchief tightly in one hand: this stood out because yellow was Jen's favourite colour.

Section 2: Those Who Raised Her

Her father was a lawyer who loved two things: his work and his youngest daughter. Jen described him as controlling and opinionated. He made the final decisions in the home and her mother, always keeping the peace, never questioned him. As an adult looking back, Jen believes her mother suffered from some type of depression because her eyes were often red from crying, she was tired all the time, and she often had a far away look. Jen said it was as if her mom drifted in and out of the present moments.

Jen was certain her father adored his youngest daughter Sue because she looked the most like him with his hair and eye colour; on birthdays and Christmases it was painfully obvious to everyone that Sue's presents from him were far more extravagant, but it was one of those things that didn't ever get talked about. Jen explained there were never any real conversations at home.

When asked how her parents affected her self-image, Jen's response was, "Well they didn't help it."

Section 3: What She Learned to Value

When it came to values, her father had a set image of how he wanted his family to appear in public: happy and well put together. He used phrases like "how would it look" or "what would people think" quite freely. It wasn't unusual for him to suggest his wife lose a few pounds or that Jen dress better. When it came to the younger daughter however, Jen said "she could do no wrong."

Section 4: Overall Climate

When asked to describe how her home life felt, Jen labeled it as lonely and cold; it had been that way for as long as she could remember. She'd tried. She used to wait for her father to come home, only for him to grab his dinner and eat in front of the TV, with the volume loud. At age 10 she used to check in on her mom who slept in way longer than usual, only to be shooed away. According to Jen, being around her father got easier when she got her degree, found an excellent job, and married a good man. Jen jokes that it took all those three things for her father to notice her, because by then her sister was on endless *finding herself* journeys around the globe.

Section 5: Ups and Downs of Teen Years

Jen reported coasting through her teen years, relying on a couple of friends for the warmth and support she craved at home. While these relationships didn't go deep, she said they were better than being alone. Jen had a hot and cold relationship with Sue throughout their lives. Their mother went further into herself by developing a reliance on alcohol, and her father was busy expanding his legal firm.

Jen admitted that she raised herself.

Section 6: Critical Events

During a family gathering while in her early teens, Jen overheard a conversation between her mom and an aunt (her mom's sister). They were talking about how Jen's father indulged his Sue, and the aunt said: "Can't say I blame him, I mean she's prettier, trimmer and much easier on the eyes than her sister." She remembered her mom, a few cocktails in saying, "That's true." Then her mom and aunt burst into laughter like it was the funniest joke.

Jen called that *the night I realized I was truly alone.* No one noticed how upset Jen was for the rest of the evening, so she never bothered talking about it to anyone.

Highlights:

When we look at how Jen's life unfolded, there are several themes of abandonment, rejection, and dismissal. For instance, it can be argued that:

- Her mother abandoned her when she chose to keep the peace above all else, especially in that horrid moment when she didn't defend Jen in the conversation with the aunt.
- Her mother abandoned her by refusing to get treatment for depression and alcoholism.
- Her father abandoned, dismissed, and rejected her by prioritizing his younger daughter and everything else.
- Both parents were emotionally unavailable to her.
- There was no sense of warmth, acceptance and belonging in the family.
- So many things could have been different if her parents had faced their own issues through helpful family members, social supports, or therapy.

Mark

Section 1: Ups and Downs of Childhood

Mark was an only child. He didn't remember much about his earlier years; what he did recall was watching his mom load three suitcases into her blue sedan. Mark was nine years old. Before getting in the car, she hugged him tightly saying something like *this is the only way*, and *I'll come back for you,* but he didn't see her again until his 10th birthday several months later.

This was also around the time she filed for divorce, and the battle for him began.

Section 2: Those Who Raised Him

Mark disclosed that his parents put him on the spot to decide who he wanted to live with, so he opted to stay with his father so he wouldn't have to move. He described him as good man, but "just one of those people who couldn't get his shit together." His father was a truck driver for a small moving company, which meant long hours and weekend work. His father changed employers several times.

Mark's mother was an office manager who quit her well paid position to raise him. He considered her a caring and strong-willed person. Before she left there were years of arguments about money, and the chaos of his father's work scheduled. Mark wondered if his mom resented giving up her career, but he never felt he could ask her that. Mark didn't believe either of his parents were ever genuinely happy.

Section 3: What He Learned to Value:

Mark learned to value financial stability. While he never got the real gist about why his parents split up, he knew cashflow was a big factor. He vowed to "do it right" someday: marry a girl he loved and have a houseful of kids, so he would never feel lonely again.

Section 4: Overall Climate

Mark talked about his homelife in terms of before and after. When his mom was there it was tense, but she made him do his homework, he always had clean clothes, and he ate healthy meals.

After, his father bought canned and prepared food. He rarely cooked. Mark noted that the house felt eerily quiet, uncomfortably so. He found it cold because when his father was home, he was usually asleep on the couch in front of the TV.

Section 5: Ups and Downs of Teen Years

Mark fell in love when he was 15; this led to a relationship that lasted most of his high school years and he was sure he'd found *the one*. The winter before graduation she broke it off, saying they'd drifted apart, so there was no point in prolonging the inevitable.

Mark fell into a deep depression for a couple of months; mostly he was angry with himself for not giving her everything she needed, even if he didn't understand what those things were. He saw the school counsellor for a while and managed to graduate with strong marks.

Mark believes his parents did their best. He said, "They were good people who let the stresses of life take them; eventually we all got so busy, and no one cared enough connect."

Section 6: Critical Events

Mark was 17 when his father remarried. His new wife owned a nicer home; by then his mom was living with a man Mark didn't like, so left with no choice, Mark moved with his father. It took him further away from his high school, and his then girlfriend. He wondered if that was part of the reason she dumped him. He did admit that all those events, the remarriage, the move, and break up not too long after just about ruined him. That was around the time he put all his energy into building his own future because he realized no one was going to help him do it.

Highlights:

When we look at Mark's story, there are several themes of abandonment, rejection, and dismissal as well. For instance, it can be argued that:

- Watching a parent leave is a traumatic event for a child when not handled well (there could have been lead-up conversations about changes coming through one family meeting even if it wasn't their norm to have one; they could have explained to him what to expect in the future and assured him it wasn't his fault).
- Even at age 10, the decision on where he was to live should have been shouldered entirely by his parents.
- His mom and dad disengaged from him to the point that he dealt with his teenage heartbreak without them.

Now that we have their background stories, let's dive into how this all applies to everything we've discussed so far when it comes emotional proximity, emotional triggers, and emotional armour.

Jen was **triggered** by Mark's resistance to finally having children. She said she felt like a helpless child again, being denied something she deeply wanted and knew in her heart she deserved. Mark was also **triggered** by the pressure he was feeling from Jen, because becoming a father meant it was time for him to face his deeper fears about that.

Jen: "You are supposed to be my safe place, the one human on this planet **(proximity)** who shouldn't ever make me feel insignificant, yet here we are. I worked so hard to have my own life, so I'd never relied on anyone for happiness, because that's what people do, they let you down. They put their needs first, and mine have never ever mattered. So, for you to just shove my wants aside, that's cruel! Did you lie when we were dating, **(armoured accusing)** all those times you said you wanted kids? I'm sick and tired of shaping and bending myself for others. You make it all about these stupid work goals, my dad did that and it killed his marriage. I'm not my mom who'll shut up and drink her problems away. I survived *them,* if this marriage doesn't work, I'll survive *you* too **(armoured threatening)**."

Mark: "What, you think you're the first woman to leave me **(armoured bitterness)**? You'd be the third Jen, because that's what the women in my life do. Leave. It's easy for you to belittle my goals, you guys were filthy rich. You don't know what its like to make one stale loaf of bread last a week because your dad didn't think to buy groceries before he went away on a job."

Jen: (Stilled, and shaky voice). "Omg Mark… I didn't know. I'm so sorry…".

Mark: (Softer tone). "I couldn't tell you, I still can't, its embarrassing. Humiliating. I hid how hungry I was because some kid at school had to talk to child services for saying there was no food in his house. Back then I couldn't call my mom, she'd just get hysterical, make me live with her and that jerk, and she'd take my dad to court for full custody. This is why. Do you see why I'm so… unreasonable? I won't let you or our kids ever wonder where your next meal is coming from. I can't have children until I know for sure we're set. I'm not messing this part up; I won't be a shitty parent. The dumb part is, well it looks like I've become a shitty husband (**vulnerable, remorse, empathy**). I'm sorry."

Jen: "Mark, you are such an amazing human (**vulnerable acknowledging**), truly. I seriously don't know how you coped in the past. My mind went to all kinds of dark places and I'm sorry I let them get the better of me. I'm sure I hurt you and, sorry for that too. I thought you were shutting me down, shutting me out. When you get that decisive tone you sounded a lot my dad, as if you somehow morphed into a selfish prick overnight. I just got so scared (**vulnerable, naming feeling**)."

Mark: "It's okay, you were kinda right. I spiraled and got trapped in my head, and I did shut you out."

Jen: "Um…I hate to bring up the obvious, but when it comes to having a child, we are a two-income household, and we're smart with money. You know that right?"

Mark: "Yeah, but babe I'm scared."

Jen: "Me too."

Mark: "Ok, can we talk again about babies in a few days, I'll feel better once I look at our numbers, just to let it all sink in. Will you humour my OCD side (smiling)? This doesn't mean I'm ready, it just means… I just understand better why I keep fight you so hard on this."

Jen: "I have to remember that you're not one of them, the people don't value me."

Mark: "Omg. Never."

Summary:

The formula was always the same: emotional proximity triggered old wounds, making them armour up. As you can see, once they identified their trigger points, they were able to lower their armour and hear what the other had to say. From there, closeness has a chance, and proximity is connection. This is the zone where all good things happen.

To be honest the cases that broke my heart the most were the ones where neither had an interest in being vulnerable. Perhaps they didn't believe they could, maybe they doubted such a safe place existed, or they didn't see it as something possible for them.

That said, the most rewarding part of this work was watching two people get through to each other in the way they deeply desired, after a long mental and emotional separation. It was like watch people exhale as one would when one is finally *home,* where they always belonged.

Journal Prompt:

Did I see myself in this example, even a little? If so, how?

Chapter Six

Tools of the trade.

More. To increase your chances of successfully getting through to each other, the following are things you can use every day. I've included images, and conveniently have them all starting with the letter "S" to make them easier to remember.

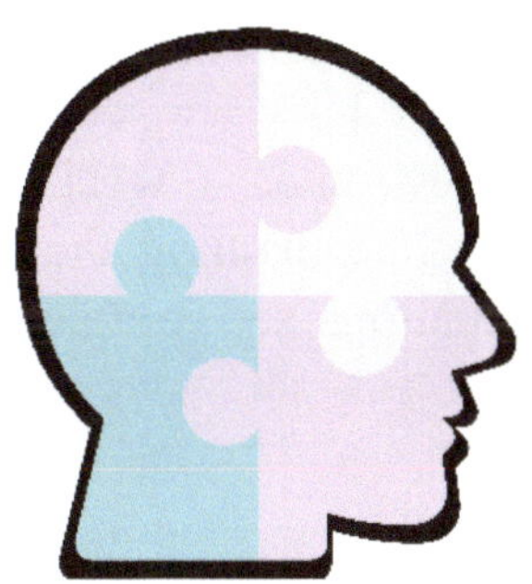

Spot the Source. When your emotions are heightened, name your feelings, and name the fear associated with that feeling (for example, fear of being ignored, abandoned, dismissed, or others). Then, search for the source by scanning your memory bank for the first time you felt this way. When you realize your present reaction is rooted in something that happened long before today, a shift begins.

Selfie Mode. This image will remind you to stop looking at your partner for change, answers, or solutions. Look within, to what's INSIDE you. Here are questions I've posed to individual partners when they swirl around in the blame game loop: 1) What are your partner's biggest complaints about you? 2) Assuming your partner is right, what can you do about this? It's time to do them.

School Zone. From time to time, do your best to set a healthier pace by slowing down your conversations. This will also slow down your racing, ready-to-engage mind; you can do this by pausing for several seconds before speaking and taking a moment or two to think about all the information before you. This also makes space for both of you to say, "Please clarify what you mean," or "Kindly rephrase." Never underestimate the power of a cleansing breath or three; this encourages your partner to do the same.

Stop Sign. There is so much regenerative power in coming to a full stop to mull things over. A quick mental break for a minute or two, or longer may help. Again, make sure to regroup and resume the talk within 24 hours so the pause doesn't turn into avoidance, which will run counter to the objective here. Don't be surprised if some discussions take several days, weeks, and sometimes months. Many couples overlook this, blaming their frustration on each other when in fact, some situations are complex and must be work through in stages.

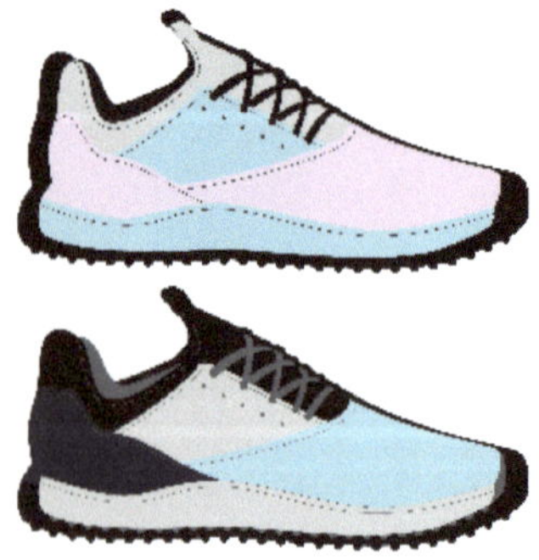

Switching Shoes. This is a serious game changer; if there are big gaps between you and your partner, it may be time to put yourself in each other's shoes and try to feel what the other is feeling. This doesn't mean forgiving something you aren't ready to or want to forgive, but it will remind you that all conversations have two different perspectives. Remember that just because you're seeing both sides, this doesn't mean you're abandoning your own; it simply means you're proceeding informed.

Speak the F Up. It falls on you to let your partner know what you think and how you feel. No matter how well your partner knows you, the best they can do is guess, and it's unfair to expect that of them. There's a high likelihood they'll guess wrong anyway because they see things through their own lenses and not yours. Your partner needs your point of view. They deeply desire it.

Journal Prompt:

What do I think of all these tools?

What are my fears about using them?

A final message to you.

I've given you a lot of information in this book, and my hope hereafter is two-fold: that you don't underestimate its simplicity nor shy away from its depth.

On a personal note, I learned through the years that I am most reactive when there are themes of abandonment; my story shaped me that way, so I continue to work on this. Understanding and relaying this to my husband helped us both; he takes all my overreactions about upcoming work trips with a grain of salt. He never tells me he has to leave until the plans are rock solid, which we agreed to, and I fully appreciate. I learned a long time ago to ask for what I need, like a certain amount of contact over the time he'd be away, which he readily accommodates: in turn, my respect for him and his overall character deepened.

Our *us* is my favourite place.

You see, when you decide to be with someone, and you wholeheartedly commit to doing it right by truly holding yourself accountable, the results will surprise you. You find yourself able to do things you never thought you could, like going back to school with two young children in tow, a day's drive away from your husband, because it's the only way everyone can have what they really need; like embracing years of deep psychotherapy to slay your inner demons with *it stops with me* fervor; like releasing a relationship book into the sea of millions to swim among the biggest names; like sharing your pain with the whole world because you just know others don't have to suffer the way you did, not if they did things differently.

I hope from my heart that you've found this perfectly imperfect little book helpful. Do let me know what you think of it because your voice matters to me.

Your relationship matters. You matter.

References:

Don, B. P., Gordon, Amie. M., Berry Mendes, W. (2023). The good, the bad, and the variable: Examining stress and blood pressure responses to close relationships. Sage Journals, Mar 27, 2023. https://journals.sagepub.com/doi/full/10.1177/19485506231156018

Sherwood, E., Dean, Y. (2021) Greatness finds a way, Alanna Rusnak Publishing, Canada.

Waite, L. and J., Gallagher, M. (2001). *The case for marriage: Why married people are happier, healthier, and better off financially.* Broadway Books.

Waldinger, R. J., & Schulz, M. S. (2010). What's love got to do with it? Social functioning, perceived health, and daily happiness in married octogenarians. *Psychology and Aging, 25*(2), 422–431. https://doi.org/10.1037/a0019087

About the Author

Elena Sherwood has a BSW from Toronto Metropolitan University, an MSW in couples therapy from the University of Manitoba, and a PhD in clinical social work, also studying couples, from the University of Calgary. Now retired with over 35 years of experience, her journey doesn't stop there. Whether she's coaching couples, leading courses, or leaving evergreen content on social media platforms, her mission to spread sound relationship advice, her way, continues. Happily married for over 30 years and has two adult sons, Elena resides in the Ottawa area.

* 9 7 8 1 7 3 8 2 7 0 2 0 0 *